Ballerina on Wheels

AMAZING AVA'S FIRST DANCE RECITAL

Written by
Dr. Cindy Zurchin

Illustrated by
Lana Lee

This book is dedicated to Ava and all current and future dancers.
She inspired me to share her story with the world.
Watching how hard she works during each of her dance classes,
I started calling her Amazing Ava.
Ava is Amazing and she is a shining example for other children
and adults to have the resilience
and confidence to accomplish amazing tasks!

MESSAGE TO PARENTS AND TEACHERS

The themes of Ballerina on Wheels – Amazing Ava's First Dance Recital are accepting differences, inclusion and courage. Below are some questions to ask your children or students before and after you read the book with them.

QUESTIONS BEFORE:

1. What do you think this book is going to be about?
2. Do you know anybody with a disability?
3. How do you feel when you try something new for the first time?

QUESTIONS AFTERWARDS:

1. List some words that describe Ava.
2. How can you help everyone in your class feel like Ava did at her recital?
3. What do you think the Author, Dr. Zurchin, wants you to remember most from this book?

This is Ava.

Ava loves to watch other people dance.

This is Ava's sister Paisley. Paisley loves to dance!

Paisley goes to dance class every Saturday and learns ballet and tap.

One day, Miss Sam saw Ava's beautiful smile!

"Would you like to dance with us, Ava?" Miss Sam asked. Ava's sister, Paisley said, "Ava can't stand or dance. She's in a wheelchair."

Ava's mom told Paisley, "Dance is any movement. Even a smile!"

Miss Sam said, "Everybody can dance!"

The next day, Ava's mom took Ava to the dance store.

Ava has been practicing with her friends. It is almost time for their recital.

The costumes have arrived!

"Put on your tutus and see how they fit," Miss Sam said.

Everyone loves their new costumes.

Ava is dancing!

Paisley shows Ava how to point her toes.

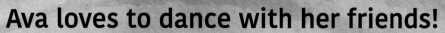

Ava loves to dance with her friends!

Ava is ready for her big day.

The music has started. It is time to dance.

Ava's arms go high.
Ava's arms go low.

Ava lifts her legs.
Ava points her toes.

Ava is happy.
Paisley is happy.

Everyone is happy.

Ava can dance!
Ava is smiling.
Ava is amazing!

ABOUT AVA

Ava is a beautiful young lady who lights up a room with her smile and eyes. Ava definitely lives life to the fullest; and her personality says it all. She enjoys spending time with her family and friends. Ava participates in dance classes at Cynthia's and plays Miracle League baseball. Ava is diagnosed with Cerebral Palsy from Hypoxic Ischemic Encephalopathy from birth, and Neuromuscular Scoliosis which impairs her ability to control the muscles that support the spine and she is nonverbal. Due to her condition, Ava has to utilize a wheelchair for mobility.

Ava does not let obstacles stop her. She is changing how people see her. Ava is not letting people judge her by the wheelchair that she is in, but for the person who she has become and strives to be!

ABOUT THE AUTHOR
DR. CINDY ZURCHIN

www.drcindyzurchin.com

In 1988, Dr. Zurchin founded Cynthia's School of Dance & Music, LLC, using dance and music to build confidence in students ages two to adult.

Dr. Zurchin received her Doctorate in Educational Leadership from Duquesne University. She has previously worked in public education at the elementary, middle, and high school levels as a teacher and administrator. She has also served in central office positions in staff development, Assistant Superintendent and Superintendent of Schools.

Contact Dr. Zurchin at cindy@drcindyzurchin.com

OTHER BOOKS BY THE AUTHOR:

The Whale Done! School: Transforming a School's Culture by Catching Students Doing Things Right

ABOUT CYNTHIA'S SCHOOL OF DANCE & MUSIC

Pittsburgh, PA

www.cynthiasschoolofdance.com

412-367-3330

Cynthia's School of Dance & Music has been helping children ages 2 – adult become confident and build resiliency since 1988.

In addition to dance and music skills, students learn self-control, team building, confidence, responsibility and to have a positive outlook on life. All of these skills help prepare them to recognize opportunities and handle the challenges they will face in life.

Cynthia's creates success, both in and out of the dance and music classrooms.

ABOUT THE ILLUSTRATOR
LANA LEE

Lana Lee has had a passion for drawing since she scribbled on her grandfather's journal at the age of one. She loves to express her thoughts with her drawings. Lana received her Bachelor's Degree in Industrial Design from Konkuk University in South Korea. She started her career as an illustrator and designer at a children's book magazine company creating characters for kid's magazines, designing goods, children's book and gifts. She was fascinated with the vidid colors and the work of telling stories through pictures. Lana's experiences led her to become a talented children's book illustrator. Her illustrations are unique and her style cannot be duplicated. In additon to being a talented artist, Lana is knowledgeable in the areas of printing and production. Lana makes stories come alive.

Check out her work at **imlanalee.com**

Contact Lana at **imlanalee@gmail.com**

ENDORSEMENT

Ballerina on Wheels – Amazing Ava's First Dance Recital is an inspiring book and a must-read for all children. It promotes the concept of community inclusion for people of all abilities.

Amy Dolan Strano, Esq. Senior Vice President – Achieva
President – Achieva Family Trust

Ballerina on Wheels is about Ava overcoming the odds and expectations given to her in life. She is making a mark in society for her hard work, drive and determination to live life to her fullest, despite any physical limitations or obstacles thrown her way. Ava shows the world to never say never. This book will inspire children and adults with and without disabilities to believe in themselves. A special thank you to Dr. Zurchin, Miss Sam, and the team at Cynthia's for instilling the studio motto of "Building Confidence in your Dancers!"

Lauren Price
Ava's Mom

LEARN SOME BEGINNING BALLET STEPS FROM AVA & PAISLEY

FIRST POSITION

Make the heels of your feet kiss so they look like a "V" or a piece of pizza! This is First Position.

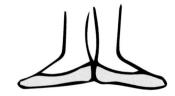

TENDU - MEANS STRETCHED

Slide your foot to a fully pointed toe to the side then slide and squeeze your feet back together to First Position.

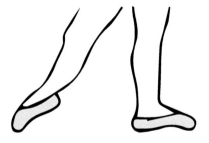

RELEVÉ – MEANS RAISED

Start in First Position with heels together. Rise up on your toes and reach for the stars. Grab some stars, hold them in your hands, close your eyes, make a wish and then throw your imaginary stars in the air!

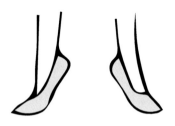

You are on your way to becoming an Amazing Ballerina too!

THE FIVE BASIC POSITIONS OF BALLET

Photos by Little Rockstar

If you enjoyed this book,
we would be most grateful
if you could take a minute and leave
a review on Amazon.
Your feedback and support of the book
is greatly appreciated.
Thank you.

Made in the USA
Monee, IL
10 May 2022